DFSolutions

4th edition, October 2019

Dedicated to...

This book I dedicate to all the people who have tried to "fooled" me in life, thanks to them I have learned how turn to "fooled" them...

Synopsis

Why can't we be rich? Why can't we all be rich like Mark Zuckerberg, who (at 34 years old) owns a legacy of around 55 billion USD? Why can't we be like him? ... but above all, why don't we give a damn about it?

We can forget all these ultra-billionaires and live in 10% richer of the planet by simply continuing our lives with some important precautions. Drive yourself in the high-net-worth individual (HNWI) club. It is not the "rubbish" of the YouTuber, the entrepreneur whit Ponzi's system or the role of bravado that will make you live the luxury...

When you are holding the reins of your life, aware of the healthy path of personal, professional, financial, patrimonial, intellectual growth, etc. you may well define yourself as a man who lives in luxury, respected and admired... and this is the only basic thing to know.

I will guide you on how to make <u>LEVERAGE</u> with the indispensable tools that ordinary life already offers you...

INDEX

DEDICATED TO III

SYNOPSIS IV

INDEX V

CHAPTER 1 INTRODUCTION TO CHANGE 6
   1.1 LEVERAGE ON AVAILABLE SOURCES 6
   1.2 RESET AND …RESTART! 10

CHAPTER 2 MAKE YOU STRONGER 13
   2.1 YOUR WELLBEING AND PHYSICAL APPEARANCE 13
   2.2 YOUR TRAINING 17
   2.3 YOUR ACTIVITY 19

CHAPTER 3 THE LUXURY OF THE THINGS 25
   3.1 YOUR WARDROBE 25
   3.2 YOUR CAR 32
   3.3 YOUR HOME SWEET HOME 35

CHAPTER 4 THE LUXURY OF THE FREE TIME 39
   4.1 YOUR HOLIDAYS 39
   4.2 YOUR FRIENDS 42
   4.3 THE LOVE 44

CHAPTER 5 HOW TO MAKE …MONEY! 47
   5.1 MEMO OF THE RICH PERSON 47
   5.2 THE BETTER END 48

USEFUL INTERNET WEBSITES AND MUCH MORE… 51

CHAPTER 1
INTRODUCTION TO CHANGE

1.1 Leverage on available sources

Why can't we be rich? Why can't we all be rich like Mark Zuckerberg, which (at 34 years old) owns a legacy of about 55 billion USD? Or as Larry Page & Sergey Brin, Larry Ellison or Jeff Bezos? ... most of which have been enriched with the "new economy", or rather with the "share economy" where, as very often happens, each of the users becomes a worker without contract in exchange for a "small service" of web hosting to enter the (their) network (or 'spider' web...).

Well,... the reasons are different and many. There is to say a truth, which may pleased or not, which is that that not everyone can become billionaire. There are physical, temporal, environmental, geographic, cultural factors, and a lot of more other smaller factors that are competing to make someone millionaire or not. No wonder if you hear from some millionaire that their idea, their product, their factory is at some point "exploded" in sales, in profits, in the number of customers. They simply were in the right place and at the right time to get that perfect mix that made them become better THAT IS. So, no wonder if someone suffers more of weaknesses or is more prone to suffer stress than other people.

And should be no wonder if an idea it would be a failure in a geographic area and becomes exceptional in another. Like no wonder if Mark Zuckerberg it became better by creating its network in the USA, in the historical moment where MySpace became more and more intertwined with the dating sites and "active" networking. And YOU could have **easily become** one of these billionaire if you had happened in that situation, driven by circumstances, driven by your ambitions. You simply haven't become it because your system is founded in different circumstances, but equally exploitable to get **your** small/big **slice of wealth**.

And so,... DO NOT EVEN CARE about these super billionaire! You can safely manage your destiny in the best way, even if you are staying where you are. You can safely reach your economic independence and be successful in the world of work, simply using the best what you already own and then be privileged to be in the top 10% of the world's most wealthy. ...is it a real luxury privilege?!

Success can come, and it will come with a lot of patience and sweat,... Should you be discouraged? No! No, because the "immediately and easy" does not exist and, in the end, this is not what you seek... and beware of those who sell you cyber finance, online marketing or other multi-level occupations that promise you to earn 10'000 dollars a day... Being rich does not mean this, it means financial stability and economic independence from others, a position of respect and freedom from the system in which you are immersed. Yes, you can live peacefully a life of luxury, aware that what you are allowing is reserved only for privileged 10% richer than our planet...

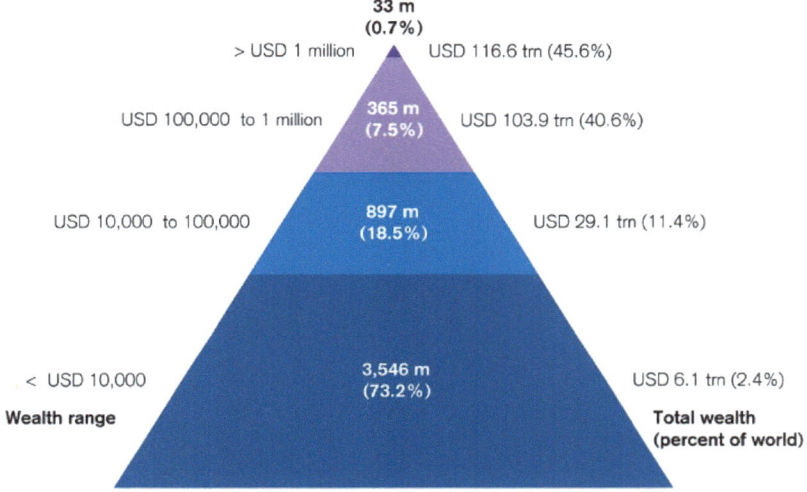

So, forget all these millionaires of which, in the end, we do not care that much, and try to live just in that 10% richer on the planet simply continuing your life with some underlined important precautions. In the end, the one that will make you rich will not be the amount of money that your company is worth (in fact the millionaires are calculated on the value of their assets, which largely coincide with the value of their companies), but will be the lifestyle, well-being , economic independence, the pleasure of security, the knowledge of ideas... and all this is a luxury for a few.

Your luxurious lifestyle can in fact become reality simply leveraging an amount of wealth, knowledge and money you already own but you're not exploiting to 100%. As I explained, you have to pay attention to the whole swindle-or "scam"-as online trading, pyramid sales, become the "character" of YouTube or the speaker of the teleshopping... NO! It's not the "scam" that will make you live the luxury... but the leverage of the things you already own, your savings, your dreams, that will increase your earnings. Take advantage of your potentiality.

And always remember that savings = gain... and gain allows you to access the well-being and small luxury that you so desire. So it also goes for ideas, your physical appearance and your security of actions.

So, when you are holding the reins of your life, aware of the healthy path of personal, professional, financial, patrimonial, intellectual growth, etc. you can very well call yourself a man who lives in luxury. I'll tell you a secret: many "rich" this luxury do not know... are simply parvenus, enriched without knowing but by the ways and thinking of the last of the slacker.

Let's see how to start step by step to build a new life, full of joy, wealth and well-being by making LEVERAGE with the little need that you already own ! Take advantage of what life offers you... **at most (!)** To get more results and you'll see how, rehearsing and rehearsing, you'll find yourself in a well-being position to envy the remaining 90% of the world. With **honesty, dignity** and **perseverance**.

1.2 Reset and ...restart!

First of all, throw everything away, or you sell everything you don't need. There are many online sites, used markets, stock-sellers and antique stores or selling vintage items and they can buy you - even in stock - all your material that you no longer use and that is only intended to fill the attics. Sell it and monetize it. It will not be much but it will be a first step towards your economic freedom.

Then start to <u>get rid of</u> all the other useless things, which you no longer use, that clutter up your space and are just a distant memory of party parties, friendships or events of your remote past. Get rid of all the superfluous, rid of these chains of the past and keep only the bare essentials, what you will be useful in your path of growth, or what is already now really useful to restart your life. So just keep the basic elements that make you remember who you are as a person. All the others, all the other things you've been sticking to or glued on, you can easily free yourself without any remorse. Get rid of it today and you're done. It won't take you more than a few hours to choose what to keep and what to throw... you'll see that of many things, in the end, only a very small part really served for you.

Then you also have to get rid of pre-concepts, common places and clichés. Very often we are victims of actions, choices, habits of the past, which we carry on without knowing why. Well: The first step is just get rid of it. Nothing SIMPLER. Free yourself of a piece today, get rid of a piece tomorrow... and continue until you have that essential. YES,... a radical change, leaving everything superfluous and breaking away from all the useless things that life and society surrounds you.

Do you feel LIGHTER already thinking you've thrown away your ex-girlfriend's picture? That you have stopped snooping on Facebook what is doing your so hated old school teammate? You seem to feel good now that you've finally letf the "boy scout" circle that you never liked, and you don't even know why you ended up in it? ...and what about that fake friend who didn't even remember your birthday? Yes,... BRAVO: throw away all the superfluous. Throw away what you were told to wear, throw away that nickname or that pattern that others had made you think you were. Do not lose time,... time run, time is money, time are occasions that run to... NEW opportunities (right away!) And leave your past behind. You are now a train racing to success! Good! **Well done!**

After you have let's free yourself of everything and all those you do not need in your life, you can finally start your life path, what you have so much desired and that for 1000 reasons you never travelled. "It's not the good time," "I don't feel well," "I'm not prepared," etc. **bullshit!** After you have left yourself of all the mental weights, induced and conditioned by the things of the past, by acquaintances, by the company and by your old neighbour's desk you will be able to take over the reins of **YOUR** DESTINY!

CHAPTER 2
MAKE YOU STRONGER

2.1 Your wellbeing and physical appearance

Well-being and physical appearance must be in the first place. Yes, because if you want to change your life you have to focus on physical wellbeing and, you'll see, it will also turn into mental wellbeing. "Mens sana in corpore sano" (clean mind in clean body) as the Latins said. And that's **TRUE!** One can say that there is a real correlation between physical wellbeing and mental wellbeing, and, from this, we would get all the strength of ideas that allow us to improve, day by day, our (your) future.

In fact your physical wellbeing will lead you to a higher concentration of endorphins, hormones, a decrease in acids, etc. there are so many things that improves with a correct and constant physical activity. This activity will have to be done regularly in order to benefit from it.

A second step towards physical wellbeing is diet. YES, in fact, as shown by a lot of statistics, researches, surveys, books, programs, etc. Most of the benefits that the body can derive is due to proper and healthy eating. Avoiding the fast-food... and if you can also the restaurants, bars, cafes and everything you find outside your kitchen at low price or "just to remove the whim". No, no, and then no! They are very damaging to your health and also to your pockets. It is in fact as overt, a equal lifestyle (sporty, semi-sporty, semi-sedentary, sedentary, etc.) the food of fasts-foods (like McDonald, KFC, etc.) increase liver diseases, increases cholesterol and fats because of oily substances, raw materials of low quality, and sauces that in It can be found. Not to mention the little time made available to sit and eat with the rest that must be.

So start, slowly (give to yourself 45 days), to improve your diet.

Do not start to eat or eat differently from what you have been accustomed to from today to tomorrow because 1. you're not going to make it, and, 2. it has counterproductive effects. Avoid false myths. It starts with the **right rhythm**, day after day, with reducing the salt, reducing the sugar, reducing the processed carbohydrates and instead increasing the white meats, increasing the legumes, increasing the vegetables and fruits.

Make a balanced diet, with special attention to take on proteins, which are the right source for improving muscles. Find out if you can, once a week, skip the evening meal, increase your testosterone levels and get even more energy the next day. Start your diet right away, and follow it for at least 120 days,... then it will be yours, assimilated into your daily routine, it will be your lifestyle.

Because after a period of assimilation the diet, like many other new things you'll find, will begin to become a habit, to become normality.

To accompany the diet will be a healthy and regular physical activity. You can also do it for FREE. These are exercises in <u>full body</u>, because it's easy, fun and costs nothing. Which is also useful for your pockets. What's better than doing push ups in the park, or a race in the mountains, or a series of abs comfortably on the carpet at home? Many video tutorials that you find on internet explain how, with nothing, with only your body, you can get results equal to those you can get in a gym equipped. Yes, because the result that is desirable to get will not be that of a macho bloated of steroids, but that of a healthy athlete.

The full body exercises will help you to head towards this direction, which is also very appreciated by the opposite sex... Then: avoid pumping the muscles until they burst but concentrate on the physical wellbeing of an athletic body. Focus yourself in <u>defining</u> muscles, in strength, rather than bulk them. Focus yourself in the proportion between body weight and fat mass and in the proportion of forms. And all this does not cost **nothing**: you only have to use yourself, the strength of determination and the gravity force!

You can start slowly, plan already today. Take a few minutes to set up your mind, focus on your goal, take time to meditate before starting the exercises and once you have outlined your goal, do it! Start and continue, with perseverance on daily-basis at least four times a week. If you can do it every day all the better, but don't overdo it! Your body also needs rest. And if, finally, you want to get more muscle mass you can always take weights to use at home. Without spending a lot of money in gyms or wellness centres: with less than a hundred dollars you find all the indispensable for lifts, dumbbells and elastics.

Last thing is sleep: **sleep is a fundamental** element for physical wellbeing. Sleep well, sleep abundantly... 8, 9, and also 10 hours per night. It is in fact known that sleep brings incredible benefits to the body and also to the mind. Especially after you have done a long physical activity (evening). It takes hours to get your body to rest properly. Be careful that your room is quiet (if you don't wear earplugs too), beware that there are no bright sources on and detach your eyes from your smartphones at least 30 minutes before going to bed. Do not stay attached to the TV late and prefer a good book to the usual tablet. Make sure everything is perfect for a nice long sleep! ...ah, I forgot, if then after lunch, about 12:30, you have time for 10 minutes of good nap do it... it's a cure for everything!

2.2 Your training

Do you feel better? Do you feel already regenerated? Do you feel stronger? Well! ...then the right time has come to add to your wellbeing routine also the training. "There is no favourable wind for the sailor who doesn't know where to go" said Senaca... and in fact **it is true!** The first thing you need to put in your head is what you want to become, which direction to take. Training will make you a specialist in a particular thing: manufacturing, banking, finance, construction, agriculture, international relations, languages, etc. There are countless areas in which to specialize, to become an expert and make the most of your knowledge. Well, it's time to figure out which way to focus YOUR TALENT. And if you're already working in that particular sector all the better... training will be the flywheel to take on a more important role, respect and better paid.

Now on the internet as in classrooms there is a multitude of opportunities to learn. Read and assimilate books on management rather than on your industry; This will be useful as **having a degree at Harvard University**. It is found that a person who studies, informs, listens, tests and tries (even failing) is able to reach the highest places in our society even without holding a diploma or a degree.

Read, inform, listen to broadcasts of interest and culture; Press the audiobooks to the usual radio; Then go to seminars and short courses; Stay up to date, study and learn. There is no better investment than in your training... This will provide you with an incredible leverage on your daily success! "Leaders are readers!" is often said ...and so: read, read, read! A list of FREE information sources of knowledge to deepen your field can be:

- Blogs, internet websites, tube channels, etc.
- Libraries, reading circles, "opendays" libraries, etc.
- Free seminars, fairs, events, etc.

...a lot of them...really many sources! ...and all these sources you can enrich your personal experience, makes them yours, internalize the knowledge in you and reinvent them, why not, creatively... in your way!

If you want a more classic route there are also training institutes. Schools, higher education courses, universities, university foundations, etc. are all institutions that at the end of a route that usually varies from 2 to 5 years, allows you to obtain a diploma internationally recognized, also by the Education Ministry. But do not focus too much on the diploma, focused on the path that leads you to this diploma. The path will be the source of your vast knowledge and your specific know-how. Then, the diploma, will be just a small "plus" to introduce yourself in front of your interlocutors, the certificate of your commitment of studies and institutionalized learning. But the true value is what you have learn during your studies.

Have you already decided on which sector to increase your skills? **...think About it! And let's start** today to comb through the various sources of information to enrich your mind and your knowledge. You will soon discover an infinite vastness of notions and concepts to be applied in your life and for your successful business.

2.3 Your activity

Well, now we move from passive gain - i.e. the saving, from investment in yourself-physical and knowledge, to active gain - i.e. the activity. Your professional activity is the source of revenue you perceive, and therefore your investment power. The bigger your income is, the lower are your expenses and, so, the more money you can put in your investments. So, try to maximize revenues as you can minimize the outputs. Find a job that lets you in a lot of... money! And if you already do not change it but maximizes your skills and make your role important. Create a method, experience the method you've seen to do by so many others who are successful, do your own and continue to improve yourself - let's improve it. Your method will soon become every day, a rule to be applied consistently and perseverance day after day. **You are a train** that marches in one direction, in a single track... towards success! The method will be your locomotive that you consent to travel at full speed towards your goal of economic wellbeing and financial independence. Continue to load your "train" with other activities, without weighing it down, but enriching yourself for every new activity you accomplish.

Your employment, your business can be of a dependent or autonomous nature. In the first case you simply have to commit yourself with rule, constancy and persistence within an organization, enterprise or entity. Start from the bottom, learn the "fundamentals" of your work and then add, <u>without overdoing</u>, other commitments, other "tasks", other activities. Build your space within this organization, enterprise or entity. Show, consistently, an improvement in qualitative and quantitative terms of your work. It seeks to become indispensable and essential for this organization, enterprise or entity. Make sure that without you everything would collapse. Take the reins of some fundamental activities and perform them to perfection.

Yes, the secret is very often to carve out your own space, then to enlarge the sphere of your activities and of your complementary and related functions. But again: be careful **not to overdo it!** You would get the opposite effect! So make the most of the task that has been assigned to you, in a precise, punctual and constant way until you get to perfection. Then also focus on the related tasks, perhaps forgotten by someone, the so-called "grey areas" where you do not know who executes that activity.

Assume a role at 360°, well connected and connected with the activities that your colleagues do. In this way your initial role will become more and more a "key" role and coordination between other functions within the company. Try, in other words, not to work "compartmentalized" but collaborate and accomplish the activities of connection between the various areas of work. Try to make sure that your colleagues and all the staff agrees that your function is a bridge, it is a keystone into the organization. Useful for the specific task you accomplish, but also useful for other activities that you refer to. An organization is made up of multiple activities. Yours must be indispensable. In doing so your role will pass from a simple performer to a coordinator-manager, with important implications in terms of salary and therefore GAIN.

The alternative... is to become an entrepreneur!

If, instead, you prefer to work for yourself, be autonomous, be a self-made-man then opt for an entrepreneurial activity. The entrepreneurial activity in the long period is that of greater satisfaction in salary terms. In fact, most of the wealthy people (the so-called "rich") come from an entrepreneurial path, where their activity brought to high levels made him earn a lot of money! Avoid Ponzi systems, pyramid systems and all those things like "sell to your neighbour or your relatives this or that package." First thing advertised: marketing is the key to success for all those who want to work "for itself". Build your own image, build your business card... publicized and sell as best you can. This will be a first step in attracting your customers.

Second thing, don't wait for the customers... try them! Valleys to find, send requests, use socials, use emails, use networks, knowledge, associations, clubs, etc. presented to everyone you can present, gracefully and sympathetically. Introduce yourself and get introduced and try to understand why your interlocutor needs you. Propose your performance, your product, your service if you sense that your interlocutor is really interested in you, but forget it if you see that it does not need your offer. Then you concentrate more and more towards those who are willing to pay you better, leaving the less profitable market slices to be lost.

But be careful not to fall among the time wasters. Remember that many will offer you to become a millionaire, a successful entrepreneur, a super wealthy if you cooperate with them... but the easy wealth that they offer you is in fact false. Instead, focus on your business, consistently, to achieve an important, constant and lasting wellbeing throughout your life. In the opposite, those whom chose to follow other "strange" adventures of imaginary and immediate successes will soon clash with reality, realizing only having lost money and time. Do not waste time with other things, there is not enough! Do not waste time on the socials but use them, for your business. Think constantly about your business.

Focus on your goal of making money, to grow your business, to make known as many people as possible how useful your business is... and you'll see how even your earnings will grow exponentially. **Re-invest**, on yourself and what you are doing. If then, at some point, you will not be able to perform all your tasks alone you will begin to need to have (valid) collaborators, a new headquarters, a new... small Empire! But do not mount your head: the greatest successes are built over **time**, consolidating the experiences. The bubbles leave them to finance. You continue to focus on your expanding business. Choosing well collaborators, suppliers and helpers and... Well, if you've come to this point, any other indication is superfluous ;)

Last thing: try to copy the successful people around you. Copy... smartly! No matter what path you have undertaken but try to copy with smart, to "steal" the secrets of those who have passed before you. BE HUNGRY!

CHAPTER 3
THE LUXURY OF THE THINGS

3.1 Your wardrobe

Who said "the cowl does not make the monk"? ...bullshit! **It's exactly the OPPOSITE**. And who said that "who is rich dress designer clothes"? ... It is not true that rich people have a wardrobe with clothes signed by Gucci, Armani or Versace. Without prejudice to the usual few billionaires, of which we do not care anything now. The rich, 10% richer on the planet, enjoys the luxury of elegance without spending thousands of dollars on moccasins or for a pull-over. So, dress with elegance, sobriety and "class".

Dressed in an <u>awareness</u> style; And forget all the passing fashions. Clothes with a <u>careful selection</u> that can also be found in shopping mall, big stores or hypermarkets. Avoid little expensive boutiques. And don't fill up on things that then end up in the closet to use them maybe once or twice. Focus on the essentials and the classic, which you never need to change to use every day without getting tired. The so-called "evergreen" is the best strategy to avoid chasing frivolous fashions that only enrich the coffers of multinational corporations and lose time in finding the latest accessory. Use your time for anything else. Use your money for yourself. Therefore your strategy will act in the opposite direction to fashion frivolity, making you save (= earn) a lot of MONEY and TIME.

The model that I propose is that of *casual business*, which will not only give you the appearance of a wealthy person, but also will be fruitful in terms of savings, wages and... love! The wardrobe of a man will create that image of wellbeing so envied. Your wardrobe can't miss some basics, which are the only things you need...

MODEL	PICTURE	PRICE
6 cotton shirts		150 USD
3 wool pull over		95 USD
3 cotton pull over		70 USD
5 Polo t-shirt		45 USD

1 blue blazer jacket		85 USD
1 trousers colour kaki		25 USD
1 paire of blue jeans		20 USD
3 trousers colours mild		75 USD
1 suit blue wool-mix		245 USD
1 suit black wool-mix		245 USD
	TOTAL :	**1055 USD**

For the shoes do not exceed until they are rightly used. It can be enough that 6 pairs and two slippers:

MODEL	PICTURE	PRICE
Brown "derby" leather shoe		95 USD
Black "derby" leather shoe		95 USD
Sneakers blue canvas		20 USD
Brown suede "Polacchinis"		75 USD
Grey running shoes		65 USD
Brown suede "Moccasins"		50 USD
Black Plastic flip flops		9 USD

Black canvas slippers		9 USD
	TOTAL :	**418 USD**

Why do these shoes with these clothes make you rich? The secret is choosing the sober classic pairing. As well as for clothes, even shoes. Shoes and clothes will give you a casual-business look just for every day, to use without tiring and not tired but especially to use, rather than forgetting in the closet... Therefore in the wardrobe of the modern gentleman there should be no more than twenty items.

And the underwear? The underwear of a wardrobe will have to be <u>white</u>, which from a nice feeling of hygiene and clean. On underwear you have to essentially divide by seasons: Summer, autumn/spring and winter. STOP. The rest are all offs who try to sell you the various multinational fashion multinationals with the aim of inducing you to buy that model or that one for an alleged fashion in progress or only because "women like it". Last thing on the tank tops: never ever you have to catch a glimpse from the clothes. For this it is good to use an abundant sleeveless for the summer and a V-neck for the other seasons.

Finally the accessories, the special items like watch, belt, tie,... the essential touch of refinement to change your look in an elegant person. Also in this case you do not need to spend numbers but focus on the "evergreen", a model that you can wear today as between 10 or 20 years without problems. Your "evergreen" items will be...

MODEL	PICTURE	PRICE
Semi-gloss leather belt brown		20 USD

Semi-gloss leather black belt		20 USD
Metal Sports Watch		35 USD
Casual Plastic Watch		55 USD
Plastic Sports Watch		15 USD
Regimental tie		25 USD
Club tie		25 USD

White silk handkerchief		19 USD
Brown leather gloves		35 USD
	TOTAL :	**249 USD**

Once the clothes are properly used you just have to change with an identical pair, without hassle to chase the last advertisement. Pay attention to this passage... in fact very often we want to "change" venture into a new look, different,... but it is a temptation! Continue cultivating your casual-business look (... at an affordable price!) and even the people around you will appreciate your <u>fety</u> and <u>awareness</u> in your clothing choices. A security that is not now is inner but manifests with <u>your</u> look, and not that induced by advertising. And the effects will also be positive in your professional activity and... sentimental!

But let's make the accounts of how much it costs us every year and remember that the seasons to make purchases are only one: during the SALE period. Why spend more when you can save money?

3.2 Your car

The car is not only a means of transport for the wealthy man. But it is a "toy", a "pleasure", a desirable "sin". The man loves the engines, the sound of this "toy" which is a pleasure to possess that goes beyond being a simple asset, an object useful for the work and the autonomous transport. The car is a luxury and a vice, and as such must be satisfied in the best way. But what kind of car suits you to get the most from driving, with the minimum of costs and therefore, with the maximum savings (= gains)?

Attention should be shifted to sports cars. A sacrifice touches to accomplish, the comfort,... but this is almost never in line with the sportsmanship. And then, we will also be happy to sit on a three-door that gives us all the look and grit of the sports cars, or on a convertible of the B segment, or on a super sport of the C segment (sometimes called "compact executive car"). But we will not go further, so as not to fall back into the "clumsy", "oversized" and... "heavy"! ... and also remember the context of the European cities and roads where there is no space and parking.

Then forget those hybrid "monsters" between a pickup truck and a compact car, or those between a minivan and a station wagon, or even those between a minibus and something else...

The car must however arouse sobriety and a hint of elegance... Henry Ford said "You can have any colour car you want, as long as it's **black**"... and the standard has been preserved over the centuries as a colour of sobriety and elegance. It will therefore be avoided any other colouring that is not black or... white! Yes, because all the other colours get older soon, and as time goes by (or fashion) it will also lower the value of your automobile.

I leave the choice if you buy it new or used but... to know that a good used is equivalent to the new. Leave company cars alone, cars with many property passes or those with more than ten years, even if new. Get a good used with a few kilometres, less than 50'000. There will not be so many differences and the savings you can invest on accessories and maintenance.

As an indication I propose 5 sports models, elegant and accessible to your wallet,... that will give you that 'extra' touch of class, a little luxury for the love of the engine!

MODEL	PICTURE	PRICE
White Alfa Romeo Giulietta		29'500 USD
Black Volkswagen Golf		28'500 USD
White SEAT Leon		29'750 USD

Black BMW Serie 1		29'650 USD
Black Mini Cabrio		29'300 USD
	AVERAGE PRICE :	**29'340 USD**

Then prefer black colour for the interiors or a sporty red. Black interiors or dark grey shades are much less likely to be dirt than other colours, but if you want to give a touch of "sporty aggression", the interiors should be of dark red. Excellent optional are also the fog lamps or tinted glasses... to be assessed on a case by case basis. Last thing (fundamental): the gear...

...which must be manual...

Then for the power of the engine the more you love the bigger sound it will be. But be careful not to exaggerate... the gain is saving! But what is the annual cost? Well,... if we calculate a depreciation of 5-6 years (more just do not keep it, especially if already used by a second owner) the cost will be about 6'000 USD per year.
P.S.... I forgot... NO ASIAN CARS, especially Chinese or Indians... no, please, DEFENITELY NOT!! The tradition of sports car is in the western world.
Thank you.

3.3 Your home sweet home

There are those who dream of the Hollywood villa, there are those who dream of the castle, who dreams of the Cinderella Castel... But why have a boat of money to shell out when most of the time you are at home is to sleep? ...good question, huh?! Yes, in fact most of the time you spend at home is for rest: Sleep, eat, lie down on the couch, shower and... sleep, eat, lie on the couch, shower,... So why have a house of 200, 300 or 400 meters square with plenty of pool when all these square meters you will never use them (unless you give to some hosting service)?

The mania of greatness, the mania of the Hollywood luxury house, the mania of the super-rich footballer's loft. All this brainwashing putted in your head that wants to let you believe in being rich, living in luxury tantamount in the great and expensive MUST be put into the bin. The true rich, the wealthy finds his luxury a comfortable apartment in town. See then the side, to descend to the ground floor and find you already in the heart of the city, without thinking of long and dependent displacements.

An apartment is the best solution for those who want to economize heating costs, overhead, maintenance, etc. While having all the comfort of a house of its own. Then: concentrate on this objective and let lose all the more expensive solutions such as Villas and Country houses (very often to be put back in renovations and modernised). Take a comfortable apartment in the city, which, by the way, will save you the consumption of the car for travel. The apartment will give you less problems and less hassle of maintenance, cleaning, renewal, etc. and so you save time and money by concentrating on your investments.

Instead of spending every day 1 hour for cleaning, small repairs, replacement of those furniture so outdated that you are at the entrance, or the curtains that have given you use your resources for the other. Thus, you will have a well-proportioned, but carefully maintained, home and all the money you save is great for your investments.

If, then, you want to stay away from urban traffic, the amount of smog and chaos typical of the local cities, then I recommend a beautiful chalet in the first suburbs. Yes, not too far from the centres and not too close to the lost campaigns. I mean... find the right compromise! Make your beautiful green enclosure to stay away from the neighbours annoying, try to choose solutions and materials that do not increase the costs of maintenance and then **avoid the big gardens**... will lose time from other things much more important!

The detached houses have the advantage that all the expenses are directly controlled by you and therefore it will save the long quarts during the condominium meetings. Plus you don't have the annoying codominances that control what you do from morning to night. But... the **expenses increase (!)** of a lot in relation to living in a proportionate apartment in the city. So do the calculations well and choose a cottage not too big. Moderation and keep an eye to the finitures,... This is the secret if you love to stay independent without having to spend a digit every year between taxes, waste, maintenance, etc. - that you must know - will all be on your charge.

The houses of the first suburbs can be easily found at the same prices per square meter of a city apartment but I suggest you see some not yet built, or rather, built on paper. Many companies sell the accommodations before making them, at a subsidised price given the anticipation of the receipts. In this way the price of your home will be discounted. But be CAREFUL CAREFUL CAREFUL to not fall into small (or large) companies that can trim the scam: Well informed, ask the opinions of those who live in condos already built by this company here, try to understand how they work and their solidity Asset. Well informed on the bank guarantees of the company, the extra costs of special finishes and whatnot. But, if you do not want to risk too much and do not feel safe, buy a good dwelling already inhabited but not too old. Preferably your home should not have more than 40 years since the last renovation made on the property. This is a fundamental point to avoid "surprises". However, I repeat once again: the single houses are a great luxury, but pay attention to the expenses that are all at your charge.

CHAPTER 4
THE LUXURY OF THE FREE TIME

4.1 Your holidays

So, here we are at the leisure, that little luxury that only a few can afford. Yes, because holidays means that you have a (good) job. Holidays is a luxury not to be brought to excess. Holidays are the well-deserved rest you deserve. Holidays are the moment when you detach yourself from your occupation to recharge your energies. The holidays are a luxury, indisputable on this.

Try to take full advantage of this moment of pause from your recurring activity. Try to <u>avoid</u> every engaging in housework, stuff or something else. Unplug your mind and **feed** yourself with energy. IT IS FOUNDAMENTAL. It is in fact noted by many authors as a moment of pause, reflection and total rest is jovial for wellbeing, health and mental relaxation. So allow yourself to relax, to free your stress without thinking about anything but to your well-being.

For the holidays there are many choices, in many places but which to choose? Well, first of all I suggest you avoid the mass periods such as August and the Christmas holidays, where there is a flood of people who flock and drown to take an umbrella or to drink a hot chocolate at the bar. So try to avoid the peak periods, where everything is more expensive and the quality lows down.

And so... BE SMART! Try to reach your ideal destination in moments of low season, where you can enjoy the beauties of the place but at the same time save avoiding money-wasting. Why pay double an umbrella? Why pay double an hotel? Why meet up with the detested neighbour at the distance of some parasol from you? Avoid! Try to avoid the rules and the Long highway queues. Never worse is the accumulation of other vacation stress. So be clever, be clever... look for the rare pearl at the time of calm at the end or early season, away from other chaos.

Then, if you can, try to find some holidays that enrich you. There are many beautiful destinations also in the art cities, or in the mountain parks. Try to see the "alternatives" destinations. These are a beautiful discovery and they can save you even a lot of money because you do not throw. So try to choose the mountain instead of the summer sea, or a city of art in the autumn rather than the ski slopes in winter, or a new year in that Hamlet close to home rather than fatigued in customs controls, bulky baggage, long hours waiting in Hope to reach the most expensive tropical beaches reachable only at the distance of plane.

And also take a look at the mini-trips that catch you a weekend or so. Maybe add one or two days of vacation and turn your long weekend into a real (mini) vacation. Often you forget places a few miles from home, rare pearls that can cheer your mood and save your wallet. Farmhouses, castles, medieval villages, culinary trips, museum tours... and the more you put it. It is the tourism to "km 0" which is overlooked but it can be a pleasant surprise, without taking the plane, without taking the cruise. So, why not try it? ...you will save a lot of money for equal relaxation.

And then there are all the other low-cost solutions. such as B&B, guest-house, campsites, caravan, camper, etc.... The solutions for the savings are truly endless. Try to get a *'little heaven'* on the Internet with attention and always **reading the reviews** of users and who has been. The reviews in fact are a great way to figure out if actually the place is worth it. Do not be fooled by photos and descriptions that you find on the website of that hotel or that restaurant. Be smart, be smart... try to figure out what's really behind it. Very often you can also find travel companions on internet, then looking for "travel friend" to evaluate and discover new places with a travel enthusiast. Get help by your friends or your love in evaluate a place. Then, if you can, bring your affections... cannot be better than this!

So, happy Holidays!

4.2 Your friends

Friends must be many and precious. Especially when they can introduce you to other important friendships to create your consolidated force group. Friends can be a very useful ally in your work. "The group makes you stronger" is often heard, although it would be more correct to say "the friends makes you stronger". Yes, because **friends** can also be close to you even in the less opportunistic moments and without a profit from them.

Therefore, build your own group of friends and try to manage the dynamics within it. Do not be afraid to make mistakes, so will always stay your friends. And it is a real good exercise also to be able to manage your relationships in general (customers, collaborators, etc.). Friends you can trust and they perceive it, stay safe. And then,... give yourself a healthy chat with your friend in the office, or a night out with your friend ever. <u>Look for opportunities to meet new friends</u> and people to increase your confidence towards others. Know how to love you and earn the friendship of others... You can come back very useful! Doing so you will learn to manage people not only in the frivolities of everyday life but also in the workplace.

You can also cultivate friendships in the prestigious clubs such as Rotary, Lyons, Round Table, etc. in which friendships are valued in important works of service to the communities. Or associations of a more local nature, such as district or township association to consolidate your relationship in the territory and in the neighbourhood. Or even circles of a cultural, musical, painting, reading, etc. etc. etc. The list is really very wide and surely, following your passion, you will find a group in which to cultivate your friendships and also YOUR PASSIONS. Look. Look again. Let's growing friendships. Nothing easier. Then these friendships will lead you to open other doors, to introduce other people and situations that will also be useful in your professional activity. Use them! Use your friendships, your network of friends to grow yourself and also your business.

Finally do not forget the powerful '*mill*' that can be friends. Laugh, joke, have fun. Experts have found that those who laugh the most increases the level of self-esteem, ability to endure pain, to cope with the challenges of everyday life. The laughter helps the heart, to relax the muscles, brain and lungs. **Laugh is a really cure for everything**! Among the various things that is good laugh is also the stimulation of sleep, physical exercise of the facial muscles, improvement of the diaphragm, antidepressant stimulation, lowering of blood pressure, increase in endorphins and even the general strengthening of Immune system. Then,... LAUGH WITH your friends.

4.3 The love

And here we are at the last very important chapter. *Love!* Yes, because love is among those important things that must be in your life. Do not neglect the affections for success, do not neglect your partners for a few hundred euros more. Find the right balance and find your soul mate with whom you share your successes. She will always be with you and will give you an incredible strength in continuing your projects and your business. A SPECIAL force. So try not to neglect your sweet half but make him thank you for your success. Give him **thanks** for the force that transmits you. Be **thankful** for the POSITIVE energy you transmit. This will come in handy in your work, in your everyday making, in the challenges you're making.

Strengthen your relationship with your partner, try to find the right feeling to lead a stable and lasting life with her. Try to find a serenity together, that right pinch of complicity that can make your "she" a real important pillar of your day. A few things are enough, small gestures to achieve a relationship of mutual trust, where you can be confident without having any doubts about it. This will cheer your life and make you stronger than many people who are abandoned to themselves.

Haven't you found your soul mate yet? What are you waiting for?! If you are still single look for your soulmate in cultural environments close to your new way of being yourself. Try to figure out who could be complementary to YOU. Try to understand what is the little thing that will make it special! Look for someone who will give you something **fundamental for you** as back-share.

Often love is friendship, but also an exchange of small things, thoughts, ideas, emotions that compensate each other. So try to find the person who rewards your shortcomings to make you strong even in everyday life. That "more gear" that can give you your loved one is easily reachable. Surely you are already waiting in that usual local that you frequent, or between the offices of the building in front, or it will be right at the stop of that bus that you never take... Your sweet half you recognize it right away: it compensates you and makes you **strong** to face all the challenges that challenge you every day. **Together is better**.

CHAPTER 5
HOW TO MAKE ...MONEY!

5.1 Memo of the rich person

Read, again and again this short manual. Maybe you missed things or you can review them from another point of view... If you believe that you have been really useful, or if you want to share this experience with another person close to you then just suggest this little book, this little guide to economic success and financial independence. And you know it: there is no more beautiful thing to feel fulfilled!

"Remember that savings = gain. Remember that you already have all the skills to realize yourself. Remember, you just need to get a handle on what you have. Remember, you're a champ. Remember, you're a wealthy one. Remember the luxury. Remember perseverance, Remember constancy. Remember the growth. etc. "...repeat these sentences to yourself every day. Repeat phrases that help you feel good. Repeat it until they become part of your doing. A reminder for yourself and a good exercise to NEVER GIVE UP in the process of YOUR well-being. A good exercise is precisely the one related to the repetition of the "must" of life. There are not, as many times said, "Magic potions" but only yourself and what you can do from the resources you have. Now you know how to use these resources, how to leverage your resources... continue to practice, day after day, what you learned. A luxury reserved for a few...

And then deepen, read, discuss with your friends about their experiences of growth. Don't overdo it and never do see that you have become an ultra-rich. You would fall into ridicule, make others move away and get the opposite effect of what you are looking for. Well-being is nice when it was achieved with a <u>healthy growth process</u>, respecting your times. So I recommend moderation for a more solid and lasting growth. You will see that the wealth you have accumulated is available to a few. A luxury. Respect this new status of yours. Grow up, fortified, become rich always remaining aware of the context, the environment, the world that gave you <u>this **special** opportunity</u>!

5.2 The better end

Well, if you've applied everything I've written, you've probably noticed an improvement in your life. Now you are physically stronger, stronger inwardly, more capable, with more friends and more money but always preserving your integrity! ...welcome to Wellness! ...welcome to the

LUXURY! Without losing your dignity, your values or your honesty. Remember that you can grow even without fooling. Remember that you can grow firmly with the willpower and the application. Nice, huh? ... no one's ever told you that before! BUT... now you know!

It's a long path that never ends. In fact, do not block yourself in front of the obstacles but endure to perfection of yourself. Money make money as the determination makes certain. You only have to continue to reap the rewards of your commitment. You can also watch where you started to see where you came from, how far you have travelled and how much you can still walk. The path you have undertaken is only a long marathon and at every step you make your tendons, your muscles, your spirit strengthens.

Surely all the way you have done to optimize yourself has also led to a large amount of savings and gain. Well, it is simply the fruit of the sacrifice and the ability to **exploit** and **optimize** what the circumstances have given you. And here you are! Good! GREAT! **WELL DONE MAN!** ...keep it up and never give up! Never! **Never!** ... for no one to quit your path... and welcome! Welcome to the **privileged** 10% richest club on the planet...

Useful internet websites and much more...

[1] https://www.ilsole24ore.com/art/tecnologie/2012-05-18/mark-zuckerberg-fosse-nato-162339.shtml

[2] https://www.bintmusic.it/divario-ricchi-poveri-mondo/

[3] https://www.adnkronos.com/lavoro/cerco-lavoro/2016/05/20/delle-opportunita-lavoro-nascosto-piu-del-conta-networking_4y2o6FWAo1ZJ60VRnTgHOJ.html

[4] https://www.soisy.it/costi-nascosti-un-costo-opportunita/

[5] https://consiglibenessere.org/dieta/

[6] https://www.my-personaltrainer.it/BMI_FM.htm

[7] https://www.ideegreen.it/quanta-acqua-bere-37330.html

[8] http://www.blogdelbenessere.it/post/1105/aumentare-la-massa-muscolare-a-corpo-libero.html

[9] https://lifelearning.it/corsi-online-gratuiti

[10] https://liberliber.it

[11] https://it.wikipedia.org/wiki/Audiolibro

[12] http://www.leitv.it/benessere/vita-da-ufficio-10-regole-per-sopravvivere-ed-essere-felici/

[13] https://intraprendere.net/2662/come-diventare-imprenditore

[14] https://aforisticamente.com/2014/10/10/frasi-citazioni-e-aforismi-su-eleganza/

[15] https://www.allaguida.it/articolo/acquistare-un-auto-nuova-cosa-fare-e-consigli-10-errori-da-non-commettere/122407/

[16] https://www.homeexchange.it/blog/5-consigli-per-ridurre-i-costi-dellaffitto-della-casa-in-vacanza/

[17] http://www.informagiovaniroma.it/citta-e-tempo-libero/approfondimenti/volontariato/il-volontariato-in-italia

[18] https://www.riza.it/psicologia/coppia-e-amore/2402/l-anima-gemella-come-riconoscerla.html

[19] https://www.greenme.it/yoga/7878-yoga-tutti-benefici

www.ingramcontent.com/pod-product-compliance
Lightning Source LLC
Chambersburg PA
CBHW040243220526
45473CB00001B/349